7 Secrets

for Girls

Simple Solutions to Survive Boys & Stay Sane!

Dari Dyrness-Olsen, MA, LPC

ISBN 0-7414-3236-6

Published by:

INFINITY
PUBLISHING.COM

1094 New DeHaven Street, Suite 100
West Conshohocken, PA 19428-2713
Info@buybooksontheweb.com
www.buybooksontheweb.com
Toll-free (877) BUY BOOK
Local Phone (610) 941-9999
Fax (610) 941-9959

Printed in the United States of America

Printed on Recycled Paper

Published June 2006

Acknowledgments

First and foremost, I would like to thank God for being the driving force and constant inspiration in my life. Without him whispering in my ear, this book would not exist.

Next, I would like to thank my editor in chief, Joyce A. Dyrness, for her talents and skills as an editor and loving mother. You are the best!

My deepest appreciation and gratitude goes to my loving and supportive husband, Erick, who continues to listen to my out-of-the-box thinking. Thank you for being a loving partner, friend, and wonderful father.

Thank you to my parents, family and friends who have supported my goals and dreams.

An extremely special thank you to Carolyn and Tanya for pushing me past my fear, lifting me higher, listening, loving, and understanding me. How lucky I am to have two such genuine friends, mentors, and role models. You are what all women should aspire to be: strong, fearless, and motivated. I can never thank you enough for supporting and encouraging me to reach for the stars. I am humbled by your inner wisdom and bright spirits. You are my guardian angels!

Dedication

This book is dedicated to ALL girls, especially my daughter, Sophie; and nieces, Kirstin, Kylie, and Kendra. I hope to inspire, educate, and motivate you for the rest of my life. Always remember to reach for the stars. Your power is unlimited!

Table of Contents

SECRET #1 – Love yourself first!

#1 – Never base your self-esteem on whether or not a boy likes you.

#2 – Never compare yourself to others.

#3 – Focus on your strengths, not your weaknesses.

#4 – Be the best you can be.

#5 – Stay true to you.

#6 – Find your passion.

#7 – Develop yourself and your talents.

SECRET #2 – Guys are like shoes!

#1 – Toxic Boy is like a pair of smelly, old, and dirty sneakers!

#2 – Beware of the Angry Boy wearing army boots!

#3 – Do not let Flirt Boy charm the pants off you in his brand new designer shoes!

#4 – Cleats are Jock Boy's best friend!

#5 – Brainy Boy, in his shiny dress shoes, could be your future husband!

#6 – Creative Boy lives in his flip-flops or Birkenstocks.

#7 – Nice Boy makes a great boyfriend in his brown preppy shoes.

Dear Girls,

THIS WILL BE THE MOST IMPORTANT BOOK THAT YOU WILL EVER READ. The information found in this book will positively affect your life FOREVER. After reading SEVEN SECRETS you will have the skills to become happier, healthier, and more satisfied with your life. During the next few years, you will unfortunately have friends who will get pregnant, become infected with sexually transmitted diseases, and be involved in abusive relationships. As a result of reading this book, you will NOT make the same mistakes that other girls will make. SEVEN SECRETS will prepare you for the REAL world of dating!

It is crazy how all of a sudden one day you wake up and WHAMMO you cannot think about anything else but the big B word- BOYS. It happens in the blink of an eye. Yesterday boys had cooties and today those cooties are looking pretty darn cute. Barbie dolls and stuffed animals are a thing of the past. You now have a one-track mind. It seems like you eat, sleep, and daydream about boys during your teen years and longer. It may be hard to remember what life was like B.B. - Before Boys. I assure you that you did "have a life" before boys and you will be able to create your "ultimate life" during boys!

After reading this book, you will become an expert on getting the guy you want and having the relationship of your dreams. Everyone who knows you will admire and be jealous of your great relationships. They will be curious to know what your secrets are. Chapter 1 will teach you how to love and respect yourself FIRST and then to set your standards and expectations high when it comes to guys and relationships. Chapter 2 explains how guys are like shoes. They come in all different types, shapes, and sizes. There is nothing worse than an "ill-fitting" pair of shoes.

After chapter 3, you will know how to flirt successfully. The "unwritten rules" of dating will be explained in chapter 4 and you will learn the difference between a good vs. bad relationship. Chapter 5 is all about how HORNY guys are. Just because they want to get down your pants, does NOT mean that they like you. Everybody gets dumped in chapter 6 and you will learn how to survive a breakup and become stronger, wiser, and better from the experience. And by the time you finish Chapter 7, you will learn how to "live your ultimate life" and be the "best you can be", with or without a dream guy.

Every day is a NEW chance to start over. If you have made mistakes in the past with boys or life, this book will teach you how to learn from them and focus on a better and brighter future. EVERYBODY makes mistakes. There is ALWAYS hope, no matter how bad it might seem today. No guy is EVER worth losing your self-respect, self-esteem, or your friends and family. As a counselor and college professor, I work with hundreds of girls each year, just like you. Through my work, I have sadly discovered that most parents are not talking to their kids about sex. Parents should have a responsibility, whether they like it or not, to teach their kids about the dangers of dating and sex. If your parents have talked to you about sex, that is great. But you still need to read this book because it will definitely offer some new ideas that I am sure you have NOT heard before. If your parents have not had this important conversation with you, I am SO glad you bought this book ☺.

After reading and completing all of the activities in this book, you will quickly find personal happiness and success in almost any part of your life. You can write directly in this book or you can use your own journal. The goal of this book is to inspire, educate and empower ALL GIRLS into making better life choices, ESPECIALLY when it comes to boys and sex. Good luck and happy reading!

Love- Dari

SECRET # 1- Love yourself first!

The first step to having a happy and healthy relationship with your dream guy is learning how to love yourself FIRST, if you do not already. I am talking about unconditional love. Do you love yourself just as you are today, here and now, no matter what? If you already love yourself, that is music to my ears! However, you still need to read this chapter because you can never love yourself too much. Loving yourself is the best gift you could possibly ever give to you. It seems like such a simple thing, but most people struggle with low self-esteem and self-worth, especially girls and women. If you do not love yourself, then how do you expect your dream guy to love you?

Everyone is born with high self-esteem. So what the heck happened to it between the time you were born and now? I will tell you exactly what happened to it. Over time, you receive negative messages from the world, the media, your family, friends, boyfriends, and significant others that chip away at your self-esteem. Unfortunately, the most important people in your life should be giving you positive reinforcement and feedback and instead they are often very critical and mean. I say, "Shame on them." Do not waste your time trying to figure other people out. Maybe their parents were mean to them and the cycle has just kept repeating itself (which by the way is absolutely no excuse). Usually people are so unhappy with themselves and their lives that they feel the need to be mean to everyone else around them. Regardless of the reason for this bad behavior, this is where YOU need to step in and take back control of YOUR life and YOUR self-esteem. We are only given one life and one chance to do it right and find happiness. No one else is going to do it for you. Carpe diem~ seize the day. Today is YOUR day, so let's get going!

HERE ARE MY SEVEN SIMPLE SOLUTIONS TO LOVING YOURSELF:

#1- Never base your self-esteem on whether or not a boy likes you.

Even if the boy you have a huge crush on does not like you, you are still a cool girl and a wonderful person. After all, you do not like every guy that likes you, right? So of course every guy that you like will not like you. He may be the first guy you liked, but he definitely will not be the last. There are many fish in the sea. What you need to understand is that it is nothing personal. Do not become a stalker. Accept it and move on with confidence. Inner confidence is what will attract boys to you. The more you love yourself, the more confident you will become. The more confident you become, the more other people will like you.

You need to love yourself no matter what is going on in your life. It is funny how sometimes you think that if you have a boyfriend that suddenly your life will get better. Then you finally get a boyfriend and you are still not happy. Most people try to replace what is missing within themselves through other people. It does NOT work. The truth is that you need to be happy with yourself and your life today, with or without a guy and the rest will fall into place. If you do not love yourself, no one else will be able to love you properly. EVERYONE deserves to be loved and treated like precious gold.

Stop reading and write 10 times below "I love myself no matter what." After you are done writing it, say it out loud 10 times in front of a mirror (confidently).

1.

2.

3.

4.

5.

6.

7.

8.

9.

10.

Great job! The more you write it and say it, the more you will start believing it. The more you believe it, the more you will love yourself.

#2 - Never compare yourself to others.

By comparing yourself to others, you will always come up short. There are always going to be girls who are skinnier, taller, prettier, smarter, richer, etc. You have to accept and love your uniqueness and be proud of it. There is only one YOU and the world is lucky to have you! Learn to be happy and accept who you are starting right now. There is no time like the present. Love yourself no matter what. We all have flaws, even the supermodels. "Perfect" does not exist. You never hear about all of the models with eating disorders or drug addictions because they are trying to maintain an unrealistic and unhealthy bodyweight. Most people do not realize that they airbrush all of the pictures in magazines to make people look flawless. IT IS NOT REAL. They just try to make you believe that it is real, but now after reading this book, you will be much smarter than that. Famous people are paid a lot of money to look good. They have personal trainers and personal chefs. They live in constant fear that they might gain weight and no one will hire them. Even worse, they are judged solely on how they look on the outside and not on who they are on the inside. Being famous does not sound like so much fun to me when you think of how many problems most famous people have. Fame and fortune always come with a price. The bottom line is that you are MUCH more than what everyone sees on the outside. You are a precious gift. Once you peel away the wrapping, the real present is on the inside. You have dreams, desires, goals, and visions of how you can contribute to the world. Aim for the stars and do not let anyone or anything stop you. Never ever listen to other people who say that you cannot or should not pursue your dream, no matter who they are. As long as you believe in yourself, you can achieve anything you set your mind to!

What matters the most is what YOU think about YOURSELF. Some people are lucky enough to have parents that tell them they are great. Unfortunately, most people do not. If your parents do not tell you that you are great, then you have to tell yourself. Give yourself what you are NOT getting from them. Chances are they did not get it from their parents. Now is YOUR chance to stop the vicious cycle of negativity. Every day you have a new chance to start over. Tomorrow is the first day of the rest of your life. You are GREAT, so start believing it!

1- *Stop right now and go find a mirror to look at yourself and say 20 times "You are great and I love you!"*

While you are looking in the mirror, look at yourself with love, acceptance, and gratitude. Keep looking at yourself until you can accept yourself unconditionally, as you are today.

2- *Your next assignment is to say "You are great and I love you" to yourself every night before you go to bed and every morning when you wake up for the rest of your life.*

It works even better if you say it in front of the mirror. This might seem silly at first, but the more you say it, the more you will start believing it. If you want high self-esteem, this is how you get it. You cannot depend on other people to make you feel good about yourself. There is no better way to start and end the day than by telling yourself that you are loved and great. Your self-esteem is growing as we speak.

#3 - Focus on your strengths, not your weaknesses.

Too often, if not all of the time, you focus on what you do not like about yourself, instead of what you do like. Unfortunately, you are your own worst critic. You know exactly what I am talking about. We are all guilty of standing in front of the mirror and picking apart every single thing we do not like about ourselves. We ALL have positives and negatives. It is time to stop the negativity and pay attention to ONLY the good stuff. Forget the rest.

Stop reading right now and make a list of 10 things that you like about your physical appearance:

1.

2.

3.

4.

5.

6.

7.

8.

9.

10.

Keep this list close at hand, so you can read it every time you start feeling down about yourself. This is just like everything else in life, it takes work.

There is NO such thing as a quick fix or a pill that will solve all of your problems. All goals that are worthwhile take hard work and perseverance. Trust me, I have had life experience in this area. That is what makes success so much sweeter. YOU have to reprogram all of those negative messages that have been so graciously drilled into your head. YOU need to set your sights on your goal and move full steam ahead, no matter what is happening around you. All YOU need is YOUR self-love and self-support to make your dreams come true.

Every time you start being critical of yourself or if someone else is being critical of you, yell **"STOP"**! If someone else is being critical of you, give them an **"I message"**, which would be something like "I wish you would not say that because it makes me feel really mad or sad". Maybe whoever it is, does not even realize how they are treating you. Maybe they are just doing to you what others have done to them.

Using an **"I message"** is a non-blaming way to tell them how you feel and that you would please like them to stop. If you start fighting with someone and say "You make me mad", then you are not taking responsibility for your part of the problem and you are blaming them. This is sure to escalate into a screaming match.

Treat others the way YOU want to be treated. NEVER let anyone treat you bad. Use your voice and stand up for yourself with an **"I message"**. Practice saying it in the mirror until you feel comfortable. If it is you that is being critical of yourself, then go find your list of ten things that you like about yourself and read them again out loud. DO NOT STOP until you start believing it!

#4 - Be the best you can be.

You need to take what you were born with and make the most of it. Start off by taking a serious look at your wardrobe. Are you wearing clothes that are flattering to your figure? Are you wearing colors that are flattering to your complexion? Just because a style or color is trendy, does NOT mean that you look good in it. Sorry, I hate to burst your bubble, but that is the truth! What you wear is a reflection of who you are and your personality. It is a way to express your true inner self. You do not have to spend a lot of money to be well-dressed. There are tons of great stores where you can buy brand names for less. In order to get a really honest opinion, invite one of your good friends over to tell you what they think about your clothes or ask an older sister or friend if you have one. Pay attention to what other people are wearing, what you like and what looks good. Buy a book on fashion or colors if you need some inspiration. Most importantly, do not be afraid to dress differently. Do NOT ever wear things just because everyone else is. If we all dressed the same, the world would be a VERY boring place. I think that it is very cool to be different. It takes a lot more guts to be different than it does to be the same as everyone else.

Next, take a look at your hair. Is it the right style for the shape of your face? Take out some old pictures of yourself and figure out which hairstyle looks best on you. A great idea is to find all of your school pictures to compare and contrast where you have been and where you are going with your hairstyle. Also, try some different hairstyles and experiment until you find the best one. Ask your hairdresser how your hair would look best. Keep in mind too that you want to pick something that is easy and quick to do in the morning before school or work.

If you wear makeup, take a look in the mirror and see if the makeup you are wearing is complementing your natural beauty or hiding it. I am a big fan of LESS IS BEST. You are young and beautiful and probably do not need to wear any makeup. But if you do, make sure it is making you look your ultimate best and accentuating your inner beauty.

Now, what about your body? What kind of shape is it in? Are you overweight? Ideally, you should be exercising at least 3-5 times per week. This is the only body you will ever have. It is your vehicle through life. Your body is a temple and you need to worship it, love it, appreciate it, and take good care of it. If you have not been exercising regularly, join aerobics, a dance class or call up your good friend and start walking together. It is so important to keep your body healthy inside and out. Start with small goals and work your way up. For example, commit to walking twice a week, instead of everyday. Once you walk twice a week for a few weeks, then increase the amount to three times a week. As you achieve these small goals, your self-esteem will keep getting higher and higher. Sometimes people set their goals too high (like exercising everyday). They end up failing and feeling more miserable about themselves than when they started. Do not make this same mistake.

What kinds of foods are you putting into your body? *Oprah Winfrey says that "it is true that you are what you eat, what you think, what you believe, what you do. Eating well, making healthy choices, delicious choices, enticing choices is symbolic of how you treat yourself, and it shows. Your skin, your hair, your eyes, your energy level, your attitude are all affected by what you ingest".* Are you making healthy choices for lunch at school or are you going for the burger and fries? The best foods to eat are those that are not processed, like the burger and fries. If you do not believe me, then go to the video store and rent "Super Size Me". You might think twice about eating fast food again. And by the way, DIETING DOES NOT WORK.

You have to develop a healthy way of life that you can stick with FOREVER. Once you stop a diet, you will gain the weight back plus more. Eating healthy sandwiches, salads, fruits and vegetables is your best bet. Lunches that you bring from home will be A LOT healthier than what they are serving at school. Go pack your lunch right now for tomorrow.

Listen to your body and only eat when your body is truly hungry, not when you are sad or mad. Eating when you are sad or mad is called emotional eating. When you are sad or mad, write in your journal, go for a walk, take a bubble bath, but do NOT punish your body. The more you overeat, the more weight you gain. The more weight you gain, the worse you will feel. This will lower your self-esteem and will NOT help you meet your dream guy!

To make sure you are getting all of your vitamins and minerals you should be taking a multi-vitamin every morning. Are you drinking lots of water? Experts say we need at least 8 glasses of water per day. Water flushes all of the toxins out of your body, clears up your skin and complexion, and gives your body nourishment. If you want to make those pimples go away, start drinking lots of water and eating healthy foods.

Are you getting 8 hours of sleep per night? During your teen years your body is working overtime growing and changing and needs extra sleep. Is your bedroom a peaceful and comfortable place? If you have too much stuff in your room, it could be distracting you from getting a good night's sleep. Buy a book on feng shui, which is the Ancient Chinese art of creating peace and balance in your life and home. This will help give you some creative ideas about how to arrange your room. Our bodies and brains need sleep in order to function properly. At night, a great idea is to write in a journal and get your mind completely clear before you close your eyes and try to fall asleep.

Sometimes when you have low self-esteem and you do not feel good about yourself, you stop taking care of your body. You might start gaining weight, abusing drugs, alcohol, or food. You might also unnecessarily pierce or tattoo your body. Remember that your body is a temple. It is the ONLY ONE you will ever have. So wake up and smell the coffee. The better you look, the better you feel. When I was in college I went through a period of piercing my body. I regret that now because it has left scars that will NEVER go away, even after plastic surgery. I also know quite a few people who got tattoos when they were younger and now wish they had not. It is A LOT more painful and more expensive to remove a tattoo than to get one. Please think twice about permanently damaging your body. There are many OTHER ways to make a statement and develop your identity. Give yourself a complete health and beauty makeover today. Get a group of friends together and have a makeover party. Transform yourself into the REAL you, who is beautiful inside and out. Start taking small steps to making BIG changes in your life today. You can do it!

#5 - *Stay true to you.*

Listen to your inner voice. Quiet your mind and get connected to your feelings and your thoughts. When you are lying in your bed at night, what is going through your mind?

Answer the following questions in order to get to know the true you:

Who is the real you?

What do you want out of life?

Are you proud of whom you are becoming?

What makes you sad?

What makes you mad?

What are you afraid of?

What makes you happy?

What are your goals?

What are your dreams?

What is your ultimate job or career?

Again, writing in a journal is a great way to get in touch with your true self and your inner voice. Once you discover the REAL you, do not be afraid to stick to your values and NEVER let anyone pressure you into doing something that you do not want to. Just because everyone else is doing whatever it is, does NOT mean that you have to. If they are truly your friend, they should respect your choices and decisions. If they do not support you, then they are NOT worth having around. You are the one who has to look yourself in the mirror at the end of the day. Are you proud of what you are looking at? If not, you better get to work. Every day we have a new chance to start over. Today is YOUR day! ☺

#6 - Find your passion.

Everyone needs to find their inner passion in life. When you are passionate about life, other people are passionate about you.

Take a few minutes to answer the following questions:

What do you love to do?

What are you passionate about?

What did you love to do when you were younger?

What are your hobbies?

What are you good at?

What can you picture yourself doing as a job in the future?

What is your dream job?

Now take a look at all of your answers and figure out how you can make money doing what you love. Does someone you know have a really cool job? Go to work with them for a day or a few hours and learn about what they do. Volunteer or get a part-time job doing something that you love. Start researching different types of jobs on the internet. You will work most of your life and you need to do something that you love. I always said when I was young that I would be a teacher during the school year and a writer over the summer. Oddly enough, I am a college professor, a counselor, and a writer. And I love it! Follow your passions and it will not seem like "work". Even better, you will be making money doing something that you enjoy. Again, do NOT listen to what other people think you "should" do as a career. Follow your dreams and goals. These other people need to live their own lives, not YOURS.

#7 - Develop yourself and your talents.

Now is the time to take advantage of the fact that you are young and you should not have too many responsibilities. Lucky you! As a result, you can use your free time to develop yourself into a REALLY interesting and fun person. When you get older, free time is a commodity and you will not have much of it. You have to work to pay the bills and take care of yourself and your future family. That does not leave a lot of free time for fun or hobbies. My point is that NOW is the time to get active and explore all of your opportunities. Join clubs, take fun classes, or lessons in something that you think you would like. The more interesting things you do, the more interesting you become and the more you have to talk about with other people, especially guys. The more you develop yourself, the higher your self-esteem will be. The higher your self-esteem is the better choices you will make when it comes to boys, dating and life.

Write down at least 2 new things that you can sign up for such as pottery classes, dance, book club, archery, stained glass, etc:

1.

2.

Next write down a list of 10 activities that you are good at like math, soccer, dance, art, etc:

1-

2-

3-

4-

5-

6-

7-

8-

9-

10-

.

      Great job! Now go out there and actually sign-up for these new activities as soon as you possibly can. There is no time like the present.

SECRET # 2 – Guys are like shoes!

Yes, I said guys are like shoes. Guys are like shoes because they come in all different sizes, shapes, and colors. You have to try on many different pairs before you find the right fit for you! Now that you have learned about the importance of loving yourself before having a relationship with someone else, you are ready for the next step. The second secret is learning how to understand the opposite sex. Knowledge is power. The more you get inside a guy's head, the more successful you will become at winning him over and having the relationship you want.

The first thing you need to know is that men are from Mars and women are from Venus. WE COULD NOT BE MORE DIFFERENT IF WE TRIED. Girls are emotional and guys are not. Society teaches boys that they are not allowed to be emotional. If they break down and actually show their emotions, especially by crying, they are labeled a sissy (among other things). That makes the job as their girlfriends so much harder. Girls love romance and talking about their feelings and guys do not. Of course there are exceptions to every rule, but emotional guys are hard to find.

Guys are physically connected to the world. They think with their head, but not the one that is on top of their shoulders (if you know what I mean ☺)! This is especially true when guys are teenagers. They are in the height of puberty and their testosterone has made them a prisoner in their own body. During puberty, your bodies are changing and your hormones are raging. I like to compare puberty to animals in heat, except that boys are on FIRE. The bottom line is that GUYS ARE HORNY (See chapter 5 for more details). Their ultimate goal is to have sex anywhere, anytime, with anyone. I have heard it first-hand from all of my students and clients- guys and girls. I also know this to be true from my own personal experiences. Unfortunately that does not change, even after guys leave puberty. That pattern of behavior usually continues for the REST of their lives. Horny boys turn into horny men. Once you come to terms with that fact, you will be WAY AHEAD in the game of love.

There are all different types of guys, but the one thing they ALL have in common is their raging hormones. Let's talk about the different kinds of guys out there. We will start with the worst and work our way to the best. Please keep in mind that some guys may fall into more than one category. There is always a gray area no matter what the subject. But, no matter what category your guy falls into, the most important quality he needs to have is that he treats you like precious gold. Healthy relationships should make you feel good inside, NOT bad.

#1 – Toxic Boy is like a pair of smelly, old, and dirty sneakers!

Everybody can relate to having a pair of smelly, old, and dirty sneakers. This is the pair of shoes WAY in the back of your closet that need to be tossed into the garbage IMMEDIATELY. They are stinking up your life! So who is the toxic boy and where does he come from? Well, the toxic boy usually comes from a toxic family, meaning that they have A LOT of problems. Toxic boys come in all shapes and sizes. Looks might be deceiving because they might be punk, preppy, gothic, or just a normal looking type of guy. But this bad boy is rebellious and is out for a cheap thrill. He usually drinks, smokes, has unprotected sex, and basically gets himself into a lot of trouble. He loves indulging in risky behavior and will suck you in with any chance he can get.

Toxic boy may seem adventurous and exciting at first glance, but trust me he is NOT. When he starts putting your life and future at risk, all of a sudden he is not so romantic anymore. This type of boy is probably heading down the road to becoming an alcoholic, drug addict, or convict as an adult and leaving a trail of pregnant girls along the way. That is NOT so fun or sexy. His family has so many problems that they cannot or do not know how to be good parents. Toxic boy usually does not respect his mother or women in general for that matter. If he did, he would treat them with more respect.

Usually toxic boy is jealous, possessive, and chances are he is probably a cheater too. Here is a little tip: When guys accuse you of cheating, that means they are the ones who are doing the cheating. They are afraid that you are doing the same thing that they are. JEALOUSY DOES NOT MEAN THAT HE LOVES YOU. Toxic boys can look you straight in the eye and lie like they have never lied before without thinking twice. Do not be naive. Sometimes toxic boys can be verbally or physically abusive. Get out of the relationship IMMEDIATELY if that is happening. If you do not know how to get out of an abusive relationship, talk to your parents, older siblings, a relative, a guidance counselor, or ANYONE that will listen and help.

No one EVER deserves to be treated badly. Toxic boy definitely does NOT want you to be happy and successful or do anything where you might meet new people. He wants to keep you in a locked box. You need to be there when he calls. If not, he will ask you fifty questions and yell at you if you did not answer. He wants to control your EVERY move. Toxic boys will eventually try to take you away from your family and friends. He wants you to spend ALL of your time with him. Life rule #1- NEVER dump your girlfriends for a guy. Guys come and go, but friends can last forever. THIS IS NOT LOVE GIRLS. WAKE UP AND GET THOSE SMELLY, OLD, AND DIRTY SNEAKERS OUT OF YOUR LIFE!

Toxic boy is the type of guy your father will hate, with very good reason, for your safety. Please do NOT date toxic boy and if you already are, dump him NOW! Stop the insanity. You are WAY too good for a smelly boy like that. You are better off being alone. If you think you can change toxic boy, YOU CANNOT. He had problems way before he knew you and he will have problems way after you are gone. His problems have NOTHING to do with you, so do not even get involved. If you are or have been, it is time to take a good look at yourself and your life. Ask yourself the question WHY you would put yourself in a toxic situation like that? Go immediately back to chapter 1 and work on loving yourself FIRST.

#2 - Beware of the Angry Boy wearing army boots!

Angry Boy in his army boots is angry at the world. The world is his enemy. The root of his anger stems from his bad childhood and problems with his family. Maybe his parents physically abused him growing up or ignored him. Who knows? But Angry Boy has not dealt with the cause of his problems yet. As a result, he is taking his anger out on the rest of the world. He hates society as a whole, maybe with very few exceptions, like his 95 year old grandmother who is nice to him. He is a social outcast. He is only friends with other social outcasts. You will find him bad-mouthing and criticizing mostly everything and everyone he encounters. Nothing positive EVER comes out of Angry Boy's mouth. He thinks negatively, talks negatively, and acts negatively. He is a time bomb ready to explode at any given minute and hopefully you will not be anywhere near him when he does. It is not a question of WILL he explode, it is a question of WHEN?

Angry Boy goes straight home after school in his army boots of course and starts playing his violent video games, pretending the characters in the game are people at his school who were mean to him that day. Angry Boy has played so many hours of violent video games that he has a big problem distinguishing fantasy from reality. When he is done playing his violent video games, then he puts in a violent video to watch. A good indicator if you are dealing with an Angry Boy is if his own mother is afraid of him. She cannot control him anymore because he towers over her physically.

Remember Columbine? Those were good examples of Angry Boys. Do NOT be fooled. Angry Boys are dangerous. If they do NOT get help, they will definitely become a threat to society. If they DO get help from a professional counselor, there is a chance for a happy ending. But until then, my advice is to stay FAR away from Angry Boy until he trades in his army boots for a classier pair of shoes!

#3 – Do not let Flirt Boy charm the pants off you in his brand new designer shoes!

Flirt Boy is the smooth talker and the guy who flirts with anyone and everyone. He loves the thrill of the chase. He is VERY well-dressed, with impeccable taste. He can talk the talk and walk the walk in his brand new designer shoes. The problem is that he is just TOO put together. Just call him Mr. Romance. He is trying to sweep you off your feet, as well as ten other girls at the same time. But he is SO smooth that no one knows just how many girls he is flirting with at once. He makes you feel like you are the ONLY girl that exists on his planet. YEAH RIGHT!

Do NOT think you are special because he is paying attention to you. You know what they say about practice makes perfect? Well, Flirt Boy is just trying to perfect his technique. He thinks it is a challenge if you do not reciprocate his advances, so it makes him try even harder. But it is NOT because he wants you in particular. He just wants to be successful at his conquest. You are just another notch on his belt. Obviously, THIS IS NOT THE TYPE OF GUY YOU WANT TO DATE. You CANNOT trust him or change him. It has nothing to do with you. He will NEVER be satisfied with just one girl. He wants a whole harem. Once a flirt, always a flirt is a tried and true motto with Flirt Boy.

Chances are that Flirt Boy will stay a flirt no matter how old he gets and even after he gets married. By then he will have a whole closet full of new designer shoes and outfits to match. I pity his poor wife because he constantly needs his ego stroked by other women. He can never get enough validation that he is attractive to the opposite sex or that he "still has it". Whatever "it" is? Why does this happen you ask? Because he has such low self-esteem and does not even know it. He needs other people to tell him how great he is in order to get through life. He thinks he is DON JUAN, but in reality he is a BIG LOSER. Do not get sucked in by this type of guy. After all, who wants to have to share THEIR man?! If you meet a guy in brand new designer shoes, put your sneakers on and start running FAST!

#4 – Cleats are Jock Boy's best friend!

Everyone knows the Jock Boy type. He spends ALL of his time eating, breathing, and sleeping in his cleats. When he is not playing sports, he is hanging around with "the boys" on the team. While sleeping he is dreaming about scoring the winning point, as the stadium goes wild and he is the team hero. During meals he is bulking up for the "big game". More times than not, you can find Jock Boy in the gym pumping iron and admiring his big biceps in front of the mirror. He worships his varsity jacket and cleats and will probably have them bronzed after high school. He is obsessed with the game. He loves to watch sports on television. Most Jock Boys even bet on sports, which could be the first stage of an addiction to gambling.

If you are the girlfriend of a jock, you are lucky if he can find time for you. You might start thinking that you are just "arm candy" for when he needs to have a date for a party or a pep rally. And you are NOT ONLY dating him, you feel like you are dating the WHOLE team too. They come as one big package. And watch out if the boys decide that they do not like you, you are usually kicked to the curb and dumped. Even if Jock Boy does really like you, he cannot openly admit it because then he would not be cool. Do NOT waste your time with the jock because he does not have the time for you! After all, you should NOT have to compete for his affection against a leather football or baseball. Chances are also slim that he will become a professional athlete in the future. The only positive thing I can see that might come from dating Jock Boy is that your social status might get bumped up a few notches, but IS IT REALLY WORTH IT?

#5 – Brainy Boy, in his shiny dress shoes, could be your future husband!

Brainy Boy may not be the cutest or the coolest in his shiny dress shoes and well-tailored suit, but trust me he will probably end up the RICHEST and most SUCCESSFUL. He dresses for success. He focuses on the position he wants in life, not in high school. He is probably the President of the Future Business Leaders of America Club. At your 5 or 10 year class reunion, you will be talking to him and thinking "why didn't I marry Brainy Boy instead of Jock Boy?" (Dress shoes go with many more outfits than muddy cleats.)

Brainy Boy takes his studies and future very seriously. He goes to every class and takes very thorough notes. He does his homework every night and always hands it in on time, if not early. Learning new things excites him.

This seriousness will reap many benefits later on in life when he can buy the car and house of his dreams. Brainy Boy has an entrepreneurial spirit and may already be running his own profitable business on the side. He is DEFINITELY quite the catch.

Brainy Boy has very clear goals and is not willing to let cliques or chicks get in his way. He may not even be interested in girls at this point in time because he does not want to get distracted. But keep this in mind when you attend your class reunion some day or when you are bored and staring at his shiny dress shoes in class. Brainy boy will probably have blossomed into a good-looking and very successful man. You better snap out of it and compliment his shiny dress shoes before someone else does!

#6 - Creative Boy lives in his flip-flops or Birkenstocks.

Creative Boy might be into music, art, theater, photography or writing. He is wearing very comfortable shoes or no shoes at all. He wants to feel free in his flip-flops or Birkenstocks and not constricted. He might be the lead singer in a band, a painter, or a poet. Creative Boy is a VERY deep guy and in touch with his emotional side. That is where his creativity comes from. He is in tune with his inner self. As long as he treats you like precious gold, he can be a very cool guy to date. Who knows? You might even get a poem or song dedicated to you one day.

Creative Boy walks to the beat of his own drummer. He is NOT concerned about conforming to society's expectations. Personally, I think that is really cool. It takes A LOT of courage not to be like everyone else. Creative Boy is NOT afraid to be different. If anything, he thrives on it. He is striving to be one with the universe. All kinds of different things inspire him, maybe even you! He loves to brush your hair or read you poetry at the beach. Creative

Boy is romantic in every sense of the word. He might even be famous someday and then you could say that you dated him in high school. Who knows, maybe you will be interviewed one day for dating the now famous Creative Boy?!

#7 – Nice Boy makes a great boyfriend in his brown preppy shoes.

Nice Boy is the BEST catch in town with his brown preppy shoes. If you have not realized it by now, it is pretty hard to find nice guys these days. So when you do, hang on tight. Nice Boy comes from a very happy and healthy family. He loves his mom more than anything in the world and treats her with utmost respect. That is a good sign because that means he will treat YOU with respect. Nice boy's mom definitely taught him how to treat a girl right. If you get the opportunity, you might want to thank her for doing such a great job.

Nice Boy actually has GOOD manners! He will hold the door for you, wait for you after class, carry your books, and many other thoughtful things. He will actually take you on a "real date" and pay the bill. Nice boy gets along well with your friends and family. He is also willing to wait, even though he may not want to, if you are not ready to have sex. He respects that you have a mind of your own and actually encourages it. And if he does not do all of these things for you already, he will not get offended if you tell him that is what you want him to do. This is because Nice Boy knows how to communicate and also listen. His social skills are top-notch.

Nice Boy has set high goals for himself and his future. He wants to attend college and have a successful career. He is also involved in a lot of activities, whether it is clubs or sports. In conclusion, Nice Boy makes a GREAT boyfriend! We ALL deserve to be treated with respect and this is the guy who will do it. If you cannot bring home your new guy to meet mom and dad, it means he is NOT the kind of guy you should be dating.

Now take a minute and create a profile of your "dream guy". The more specific you are about what you want, the better chance you will have to find your dream guy.

Please answer the following questions:

1. What kind of shoes will your dream guy wear?

2. What does your dream guy look like? (Hair color, eye color, build, height, weight, etc)

3. How would he treat you?

4. What kind of morals and values would he have?

5. What hobbies would he have?

6. *What type of family would he have?*

7. *What religion would he be?*

8. *What kind of music would he listen to?*

9. *What kind of sports does he like?*

10. *How would he dress?*

11. *What kind of car would he drive?*

12. *What kind of job would he have?*

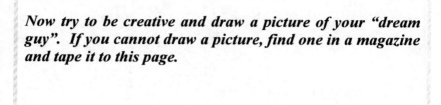

Now try to be creative and draw a picture of your "dream guy". If you cannot draw a picture, find one in a magazine and tape it to this page.

After reading this chapter, you should have a crystal clear picture of the type of dream guy that you want. You are on your way to personal success and happiness and ready to learn Secret #3!

SECRET # 3 –Flirting is an art!

So far you have learned that you must love yourself FIRST before having a successful and healthy relationship with your dream guy. You are now an expert on the types of guy's shoes that are out there and you have created a detailed profile in your head and on paper of your dream guy. Now you are ready to learn Secret #3- flirting is an art.

Flirting is a universal part of human nature and has been since the beginning of time. Flirting is truly an art because it is VERY different for everyone. What might work for you, might not work for someone else. You might not be comfortable with doing the hair flip, but your best friend is an expert at it. That is okay because by the end of this chapter you will figure out what you can do instead, that is just as, if not more effective. The most important thing to remember is to BE YOU. Flirting is the first step to letting someone know that you are interested in them. If they are interested in you, they will flirt back. If not, NO big deal. You will just have to move onto the next dream guy.

When you first meet new people, their initial impression of you will be based mostly on your appearance and body language, next on your style of speaking and last on what you actually say. People make a first impression of you within the first few seconds of contact. You NEVER get a second chance to make a good first impression. Successful flirting can put you in a good mood, increase your self-esteem, and maybe even get you a date for this weekend!

HERE ARE MY SEVEN SIMPLE SOLUTIONS TO SUCCESSFUL FLIRTING:

#1 - *Flirting is a skill, just like riding a bike. The more you practice, the better you get.*

Just like anything else in life, the more you practice something, the better you get. Flirting is a universal signal that says you are approachable, friendly and are showing some interest in that other person. It gives you a chance to see if the other person is interested in you WITHOUT having to embarrass yourself by asking them out. This way if you get rejected, it is NOT a big deal. You NEVER even have to admit that you flirted in the first place. Successful flirting sends the message that you are a friendly, outgoing and fun person. Start off small and before you know it, flirting will become second nature.

When picking your dream guy, you need to be realistic. Start off by flirting with guys who are at the same level of physical attractiveness as you. Some girls also swear by picking a guy a little less attractive than you in order to feel more secure in the relationship. That choice is up to you. Research shows that relationships where one partner is much more attractive than the other tend to end in a breakup. The more evenly matched couples are in their attractiveness, the more likely they are to stay together and be happy with each other.

There are important unwritten rules of flirting that ALL girls should follow while playing the dating game. First, do NOT flirt with someone who is already taken. For example, someone who is off-limits would be your best friend's boyfriend or even a stranger's boyfriend. You would NOT want someone flirting with your boyfriend, so please do NOT flirt with theirs. Girls need to stick together and support each other, NOT work against each other.

Secondly, do NOT flirt with someone who is a lot older than you. An example of someone who is off-limits would be your teacher or your coach. If an older guy is interested in you, do NOT be flattered. They are hoping you are young and naïve. They want sex and NOTHING more. They may say or act like they want more, but trust me they do NOT.

Thirdly, make sure that you are flirting at an appropriate time and place. You do not want to flirt during a math test or your teacher might think that you are trying to cheat. Flirting is NOT worth getting detention or failing your test. Your education is your ticket to personal success, not guys! Guys are a dime a dozen, but your life and future are not. NEVER put your future at risk for a guy, it is NOT worth it.

#2 – Confidence is cool!

There is nothing more attractive than a girl with confidence. Even if you are not the most confident person on this earth, start pretending that you ARE. Before you know it, you will start believing it. Always keep your head held high, chin up, shoulders back and walk with confidence. Be proud of who you are today and who you will become in the future. NEVER let anyone make you feel bad about yourself. YOU ARE GREAT, so start acting like it!

Treat your dream guy like you would treat your brother, even though we know that he is SOOO not your brother. Your friendly and relaxed attitude will make him feel totally comfortable talking to you and hanging out with you. Just remember, he is just as nervous as you, if not more. If you act nervous, then he will be nervous too and he will not feel comfortable being around you. Be sure that your dream guy is treating you like a girl and not just like one of his guy pals. Show him that you are NOT just an average girl and that you ARE unique in every sense of the word.

Act like he is REALLY interesting, even if you are not sure yet. Give him a few compliments. Guys eat that up. Compliments feed their egos. This is also an opportunity for you to show yourself off. Focus on all of your positive qualities. Let him know what a lucky guy he is to know you. Really strut your stuff and be proud of who you are.

#3 - *You know a guy is flirting with you when....*

- He stares and makes eye contact with you a lot.

- He smiles at you, but does not say anything at first.

- He picks on you or teases you.

- He tries to make you laugh and jokes around with you.

- He gives you compliments.

- He starts asking around about you and if you have a boyfriend.

- He starts e-mailing or instant-messaging you.

- He calls or text-messages you.

- He starts showing up at all of the places where you are.

- His voice gets deeper when he is talking to you.

- He puts his hands in his pockets when you are talking because he is nervous.

- He might blush or look nervous.

#4 - *You know you are flirting with him when*......

- You find yourself staring and making eye contact with him as much as possible.

- You smile at him a lot.

- You hang on his every word and act really interested.

- You giggle and laugh nervously.

- You do the hair flip or comb your fingers through your hair.

- You suddenly get nervous when he is in close proximity.

- Your cheeks get flushed and you start to sweat.

- You always try to look your best when you know he will be passing by.

- You start asking around about him and if he has a girlfriend.

- You find out his screen name and read his profile on the internet. You read his online journal if he has one.

- You try to "accidentally" bump into him every chance you get (meanwhile you have secretly memorized his schedule ☺).

#5 - *Do your background research and get to know your dream guy.*

Learn everything you can about your dream guy. The more you know about him, the more successful your outcome will be. The goal is to find what you have in common with him. Similar hobbies and interests are the best characteristics of a successful relationship. Go find out the following information about your dream guy:

- Find out his class schedule.

- Find out where he works and his work schedule.

- Find out where he lives.

- Find out his screen name.

- Find out who his friends are and where they hang out.

- Find out what his hobbies are.

- Find out what his family is like.

- Find out what he likes to eat.

- Find out what kind of music he likes.

You get the idea. Knowledge is power and the more you know about him, the more you have to work with. Also keep in mind that it is perfectly acceptable nowadays for girls to take the initiative and ask guys out. Asking your dream guy out will boost his ego and yours, if he accepts. On my 30th birthday I asked out my husband for the first time and the rest is history. We have been happily married for several years. The moral of this story is NOT to be afraid to take a leap of faith. You might be pleasantly surprised at the outcome!

#6 - *Learn how to become a good conversationalist.*

Being a good conversationalist is a skill that will benefit you throughout the rest of your life. You have two ears and one mouth, which means that you should listen twice as much as you talk. The most important part of being a good conversationalist is being able to listen. Be careful not to ALWAYS do all of the talking and really listen to what the other person is saying. Most people love to talk about themselves. Do your research and find out as much as you can about your dream guy before trying to talk to him.

When asking questions, make sure that you ask open-ended questions instead of yes or no questions. For example, an open-ended question would be something like "What kind of music do you like?" Instead of "Do you like rock music?" Then he will say yes or no and that is it. Open-ended questions are good conversation starters and will keep the conversation going. Here are some more good examples of open-ended questions that you can ask your dream guy on some popular topics guys like to discuss:

- Sports- What kind of sports do you like and why?
- Music – What kind of music do you like and why?
- Concerts – What concerts have you been to?
- Cars – What is your favorite type of car and why?
- Movies – What was the last movie you went to see?
- Video games – What kind of video games do you like?
- Pets – What kind of animals do you like?
- Work – What kind of career do you want in the future and why?
- School - What is your favorite subject in school and why?

Practice your skills by talking to guys who are just friends, so you can build your confidence level. If you have an older brother, listen to some of his conversations with his friends and get to know what they like to talk about. Educate yourself and then ask your friends to role-play with you. Write down possible conversations you could have with your dream guy and memorize them. Complimenting him is always a good start. Practice in front of the mirror. The more you practice, the less nervous you will be.

Most importantly, make sure your dream guy also asks you about YOUR interests. If he never lets you talk or he does not ask you questions about you, then do NOT waste your time on him. He obviously is only into himself and not you. He will NOT make a good boyfriend if he is self-centered.

Avoid the common conversation pitfalls many people make by being too negative, whining, complaining, talking either too much or too little, being superficial, shallow, or self-centered. Negativity is definitely a huge turn-off. Are you a glass half-empty or a glass half-full type of person? Do you focus on the positives in life or the negatives? Positive people are always happier, healthier, and more successful than negative people. I always try to find the positive side of any situation. If you talk too much about all of the bad things in life and complain all of the time, your dream guy will start running and never look back.

Guys want to be with a girl who is confident, happy and fun to be around. Guys do not like a grumpy stick-in – the-mud. If you find yourself being too negative, make an appointment to go talk to a counselor and get to the root of your unhappiness. Life is too short to be unhappy. There are NO second chances in life. This is the REAL thing and not a dress rehearsal. Start smiling today and the world will smile back ☺.

#7 - What definitely NOT to do while trying to flirt with a boy!

Your ultimate goal should be to stimulate your dream guy with your mind and personality, NOT YOUR BODY. Research shows that guys tend to mistake friendly flirtations for sexual interest. In other words, boys think flirting is an invitation directly into your pants. REMEMBER, GUYS ARE HORNY (See chapter 5 for more details)! You do NOT want to send out the message that you are willing to hook up with him, just to be friends with him. If he is only physically attracted to you, then that is as far as your relationship will EVER go. So many girls think they can get to know the guy after they hook up with him. Sorry girls, but it does NOT work out like that. Guys are horny and ultimately want to hook up. Once they get in your pants, there is NO reason for them to get inside your head. Do not make this mistake. YOU WILL REGRET IT.

You want your dream guy to know that you are interested in making friends with him and getting to know him FIRST before anything else. Be clear about the message you are sending him. You do NOT want him to get mixed signals and get the wrong idea. Leave it up to those girls who choose to be slutty to give the boys what they physically want. You want to become "girlfriend material" not "hook-up material". Do not waste any time in telling him that you are JUST interested in his friendship and NOTHING more right now. If he is NOT interested in your friendship, then you should NOT be interested in him.

Flirting can be fun and empowering. However, PLEASE make sure that you are polite when you flirt. You should only stare at a guy for about 2-3 seconds, anything longer than that might make them feel uncomfortable. If the person is not interested or does not flirt back, then move on to your next dream guy. You do NOT want him to think that you are a stalker.

Also, PLEASE be very careful about flirting with someone who has been using drugs or alcohol. These toxic boys could misinterpret your flirtations for wanting sex and you may find yourself in a VERY violent and dangerous situation. You do NOT want to get raped or physically hurt. ALWAYS trust your instincts. If a situation makes you feel uncomfortable, try to stay calm and remove yourself from the situation as soon as possible. Most young women who are raped know their rapist- either as a boyfriend, friend, or casual acquaintance. You do NOT want to become another statistic. Be smart about flirting and NEVER risk your life for any guy!

Flirting follow-up:

~ *Find someone who is really good at flirting, watch and learn how they do it. Take some notes and practice.*

~*Talk to an older brother or friend who is a guy and ask them what guys are attracted to and what is too much flirting vs. not enough.*

~*Once you have a good feel for flirting, ask a friend to role-play or practice alone in front of the mirror. The more you practice, the better you will get.*

SECRET # 4 – The unwritten rules of dating!

You now love yourself unconditionally, you know who and what you want in a dream guy, and you have flirted your way to success. You are finally ready to go on a date! It is obvious that you both like each other and want to get to know each other better. There are many unwritten rules of dating. Dating is a good way to figure out which type of guy is right for you. The most important tip about dating is to BE YOURSELF. Do NOT act like something or someone you are not. Dating gives you an opportunity to find your voice and use it. You need to speak up and voice your likes and dislikes until you find the guy who is the best match for you. You ALWAYS have the right to say NO, no matter what the situation- whether it is "NO, I don't want to have sex or NO, I don't want to see that movie!" Guys are attracted to girls who know how to speak up. Successful and positive dating can build your self-confidence, teach you how to assert yourself, and also be a lot of fun!

On the flip side, dating can also unfortunately be a negative experience. By reading this book, you will now be able to choose healthy and positive relationships. You will know how to identify the early warning signs of a toxic and dangerous relationship. You ALWAYS have choices and you deserve to be treated well at EVERY point in your life. Too many girls experience violence in dating- PLEASE do NOT become one of them. You CAN avoid these bad experiences by making smart dating decisions.

HERE ARE MY SEVEN SIMPLE SOLUTIONS TO DATING SUCCESSFULLY:

#1 - You know a relationship is GOOD when......

The goal of dating is to find the right guy for you and to create a healthy and positive relationship with him. Relationships are hard work, but very well worth it. There are many characteristics necessary to have a good relationship, some of which are:

- He respects the word NO and does NOT try to talk you into doing something you do NOT want to do.

- He treats you like precious gold!

- He meets your parents before he takes you on a date.

- He is trustworthy.

- He is respectful.

- He is honest.

- He is a good communicator.

- He likes your friends.

- He likes your family.

- He wants you to have other activities besides him.

- He lets you hang out with your friends.

- He is supportive of everything about you and your goals in life.

#2 - You know a relationship is BAD when......

Remember toxic boy from Chapter 2? Any relationship you have with a toxic boy is a BAD one. No guy is EVER worth making you feel bad. Relationships should NOT hurt or feel bad. Most importantly, no one EVER deserves to be abused. The person you choose to date should compliment you and add to your life, rather than diminish it. My motto has always been and will always be, it is better to be alone and happy, than with someone and miserable. It is better to have no relationship, than a toxic one. Characteristics of bad relationships are:

- He is insecure.

- He is jealous.

- He tries to control you and your life.

- He verbally abuses you by saying mean things to you. Some examples of verbal abuse are calling you mean names, putting you and others down, insulting you, laughing at you, criticizing you, using sexually derogatory names, and spreading rumors about you.

- He emotionally or mentally abuses you. Some examples of emotional or mental abuse involve any nonverbal or verbal ways of communication intended to cause psychological pain. This could be manipulating your emotions, making you feel embarrassed, worthless, humiliated, or guilty. Emotional abuse also includes controlling your behavior, telling you what to wear, when, where, and with whom to go and how to act. Emotional abuse can be anything like screaming, yelling, criticizing, blaming, lying, cheating, or threatening to kill you or themselves if you break up with them.

- He physically abuses you. Some examples of physical abuse include aggression such as hitting, pushing, kicking, pinching, shaking, spitting, pulling hair, throwing objects, threatening to use weapons. Physical abuse is anything which may physically harm you.

- He sexually abuses you. Sexual abuse is one of the most severe forms of dating violence. Some examples of sexual abuse include forcing unwanted sexual actions, making unwanted sexual advances, or date rape.

- He indulges in risky behavior like using alcohol, drugs, illegal activities and unprotected sex.

- He wants to get serious very quick.

- He isolates you from friends and family.

- He is moody.

- He explodes with anger.

- He blames others for his problems or feelings and never blames himself.

Any guy that fits these descriptions is definitely NOT a dream guy. Dump him TODAY and go talk to a counselor, teacher, adult friend or family member!

#3 – Figure out what type of date you are ready for.

There are all different types of dating. Do not be afraid to take the initiative and ask your dream guy out. There is nothing wrong with taking the bull by the horns! I think asking a boy out is really fun. It shows that you have self-confidence. Remember that confidence is cool. If he happens to say no, then move on to your next dream guy. No big deal. There are a lot of fish in the sea. All of these experiences will build your self-confidence and make you a more interesting person.

Most people start off with group dating. Group dating involves getting together with a group of guys and girls and going out somewhere. There might be some people who are coupled off within the group. The nice thing about group dating is that there are always a lot of people to talk to and there should be NO pressure about being alone and doing any fooling around. This gives you a chance to see if you really like this guy before the relationship gets serious. It also gives you the opportunity to see how he acts in a big group of people. There is safety in numbers. Safe dating is smart dating.

The next step may be a double-date or just a few couples going out together. Again, this is a great idea because you do NOT have to be alone with your date. There should be NO pressure to do anything that you do not want to do. You are just out on the town and ready to have some fun. Keep in mind that if your friends are pressuring you to do things you do NOT want to do, then they are NOT very good friends. Stay true to yourself and your values.

Individual dating SHOULD be the last step. Now it is just you and him going out alone together. Make sure that you make your weekend plans ahead of time. If your dream guy is calling you at 8pm on Friday night to go on a date that night, tell him you ALREADY have plans. You do NOT want to be a last minute kind of girl because he cannot find anything better to do. He needs to make you feel important and special by making the plans in advance. Do NOT require anything less than that. Always set your standards high at how you want to be treated. Expect to be treated well and you WILL be.

Make sure that your parents know the exact plans of the night- who, what, when, where, why and what time you will arrive home. ALWAYS make your date come to the front door to pick you up. If he will not come to the front door to meet your parents, then his intentions with you are JUST for sex. Let your date know that your parents will be expecting you and waiting up for you to get home. ALWAYS trust your instincts. If a situation makes you feel uncomfortable, try to stay calm and think of a way to remove yourself from the situation. ALWAYS carry a cell phone on a date in case of an emergency. It is better to be safe than sorry.

Some fun date ideas:

- Out for ice cream
- Picnic
- Seasonal dates, such as pumpkin picking, strawberry or apple picking.
- Bowling
- Miniature golf
- Fair or carnival
- Parade
- Zoo
- Sports game
- Concert
- Lunch/ dinner
- Movies/ rent a video
- Roller skating/ ice skating

#4 – You are ready to be "exclusive" when…..

You and your dream guy have been dating for a few weeks or even months and you have been wondering whether or not you have made it to the status of his "girlfriend". Here are a few signs to see if your relationship is heading for "exclusivity":

- You have met his family. They like you and you like them. He has also met your family and everyone likes each other.

- Sometimes he will choose to hang out with you instead of his guy friends.

- You call each other just to let the other know that you are thinking of them.

- You trust each other and can really open up and talk honestly about anything and everything.

- You communicate really well.

- You start finishing each other's sentences.

- You really like him as a person and a friend and vice versa.

- You do not feel insecure around him.

- You both start talking about the future together.

Another dating tip to keep in mind is to NEVER ask a boy if he loves you. When he is ready to tell you he will. Remember that guys have a tough time expressing their emotions. If you want to tell him, then do not expect him to say it back. If he does say it back, then great. If not, then no big deal right now. Do NOT tell him just because you want to hear it back. Tell him because YOU want to express how deeply you feel about him. Be careful not to tell him too soon because you do not want to scare him away. You will know when the time is right.

#5 – Friends-with-benefits NEVER works out. The girl ALWAYS gets hurt.

When you have a friends-with-benefits relationship with someone, it means that you are hooking up with them, but are NOT their girlfriend and NEVER will be. You are JUST friends who do sexual things together. Remember that GUYS ARE HORNY and they JUST want the sexual experience without the commitment. The girl always wants more and hopes that it will turn into a romantic relationship. It NEVER does. The guy is just using you for sex or sexual favors. Once the relationship ends, it causes feelings of regret and shame, which is VERY bad for your self-esteem. The old double-standard applies- girls who have sex are sluts and boys are cool. Once you stop hooking up with him, your friendship is now ruined. You are left feeling awkward, embarrassed and brokenhearted. Was it really worth it?

My feeling about friends-with-benefits is that it is ONLY "benefiting" the guy. You MUST require more of yourself, than giving away your body so freely to just any horny guy. The more you love yourself and respect yourself, the more others will love and respect you. Our body is a temple and our sexuality is a gift. It should NOT be given to just anyone. Do not let other girls or guys pressure you into hooking up. It will NOT make you more popular. It will, however, make you miserable.

#6 – NEVER let a boy come between you and your girlfriends.

You can have a boyfriend and keep your friends when you are in a healthy and positive relationship. There is NO reason why you should stop hanging out with your friends, just because you have a boyfriend. If your boyfriend tries to get you to dump your friends, then you need to dump him instead. No guy is EVER worth losing a good friendship over. Guys will come and go, but friends can last FOREVER. If your friends and family like your dream guy, then chances are you made a good choice by picking him. If they do not like him, I would seriously reconsider why you would date someone that all of the important people in your life do not like. Looking back at my past relationships, I wish that I listened to my friends and family when they said that they did not like my boyfriend. I could have prevented A LOT of unnecessary heartache along the way.

#7 - What definitely NOT to do on a date!

- Do NOT talk about ex-boyfriends. This is the #1 turnoff for guys. Keep the past in the past and focus on your present dream guy. If you feel the need to vent about your ex-boyfriend, then call your girlfriend as soon as you get home.

- Do NOT tell him your whole life story on the first date. Save some of your personal information for the second, third and fourth date. It is always good to keep yourself and your life a little mysterious and keep him guessing.

- Do NOT keep stressing about how the date is going. Focus on having fun and being you. Even if it is not a love match, at least you had a good time. You will go on many dates during your lifetime. There will be good dates, bad dates, and mediocre dates. It is all a part of the dating experience.

- Do NOT ever get in a car with someone who has been drinking alcohol or using drugs. Call someone else for a ride. NEVER risk your life for anyone else. Speak up and say "NO THANKS- I'd like to live to see tomorrow".

Take a couple of minutes and write a list of 10 positive qualities you want in your relationship with your dream guy. (Some examples are trust, honesty, communication, etc.)

1-

2-

3-

4-

5-

6-

7-

8-

9-

10-

*** Find a couple whose relationship you admire and ask them what their secrets to success are.*

Secrets of relationship success:

SECRET # 5 –Sex is Serious!

You know that you are great, you have found your dream guy, you have flirted your way to success, and you have been on a few dates, so now what? Should you or shouldn't you have sex with him? SEX IS A VERY SERIOUS STEP TO TAKE WITH A GUY. "Why," you ask? Sex is very serious because you could become pregnant or get a sexually transmitted disease and die. It is that simple. One moment of hot steamy horniness could ruin your life FOREVER! Chances are that the guy you are with right now will NOT become your husband in the future. He will just become an unpleasant faded memory of the past. This is important to keep in mind when you are deciding whether or not to have sex with someone.

And like I have said before, just in case you forgot or skipped that page, GUYS ARE HORNY. They are in the midst of puberty, their hormones are raging, and their testosterone level is at an all-time high. ALL THEY CARE ABOUT IS HAVING SEX. Just because a guy wants to fool around or have sex with you, does NOT mean that he loves you or even likes you. It means that he is HORNY. Guys will tell you ANYTHING that you want to hear, so they can get inside your pants. And then after they do, there are NO GUARANTEES that they will not dump you and move on to their next victim (which they usually do).

Girls are emotional and guys are physical. We are wired differently, thanks to biology and the environment. This means that guys can have sex and walk away with NO emotional attachments whatsoever. Girls have a much harder time doing that. There are emotional strings attached and as much as you want to act like you do not care, admit it, you do. That is why friends-with-benefits is such a load of crap. Eventually, when there is sex involved, someone gets hurt.

And I hate to say it girls, but it will be YOU, not him! Do not EVER give away your control and your body to a guy. You will regret it and it will damage your self-esteem and future.

HERE ARE MY SEVEN SIMPLE SOLUTIONS TO TAKING SEX SERIOUSLY:

#1 – The safest sex is NO SEX! Abstinence is the ONLY 100% guarantee to prevent pregnancy and disease.

Girls often ask me how many times it takes to get pregnant or if you can get pregnant the first time you have sex? It only takes ONE time to get pregnant and YES it can be the very first time you try it. Even when you are having sex responsibly by using a condom, it can break or have a hole in it. It only takes one little sperm to meet your egg and a baby is made. JUST LIKE THAT. Is it really worth the risk? Is he really worth the risk? And let's say that your backup plan worse comes to worse, is to get an abortion. Well ladies, that is a decision that you will have to live with for the REST OF YOUR LIFE. You will carry that guilt, shame and sadness forever. And I mean FOREVER. It is the exact same situation if you have the baby and put it up for adoption. Again, you live with the pain and guilt FOREVER. It is a losing situation and you will be the biggest loser, not him.

A few minutes of horniness can ruin your life forever. You can forget about all of your hopes and dreams just because you were stupid and let a guy talk you into having sex. You should NOT have sex unless you are physically, mentally, and financially ready to have a baby. For example, say that you are taking the birth control pill and your dream guy wears a condom too. Just pretend by chance that the condom rips or has a hole in it and you end up with gonorrhea. Was he worth it? Was the experience worth the embarrassment of having to go to the gynecologist and admit that you have a sexually transmitted disease? Was that one time worth having to tell EVERY future guy you date that you are infected with a sexually transmitted disease? NO ONE is worth that.

Many girls think that oral sex does not count as having sex. You CAN get a sexually transmitted disease by having oral sex, unless you use a condom. Just a word to the wise, I have NEVER met a girl yet who actually likes giving a blow job. Also, some girls think that anal sex does not count as sex. It DOES because you can still get pregnant and get a sexually transmitted disease. Respect yourself enough to say NO. NEVER let a boy use your body to pleasure himself.

#2- If a guy really loves and cares about you, he will wait until you are ready to have sex.

If your dream guy is REALLY serious about your relationship and you, he will wait until YOU are ready for sex. He will NOT pressure you or try to talk you into having sex. He will not make you feel guilty and say stuff like "Everyone else is doing it, why can't we?" Or "It's no big deal, I promise you won't get pregnant." Or the most common phrase used by horny boys is "If you really love me, then you would have sex with me." OH SPARE ME! Please ladies, do not fall for that crap. Do NOT be naïve. Have respect for your body, your dreams, and your future. If you get pregnant, do you really think that he will help you or take responsibility for his actions? I highly doubt it. He will be going off to college footloose and fancy free. YOU will be stuck in your hometown raising a child, BY YOURSELF every single day for the rest of your life. You can kiss going away to college goodbye.

Sometimes guys will try to make you feel bad by saying that they have blue balls. GIVE ME A BREAK! The state of his balls is NONE of your concern. Tell him to go take care of his own balls. Do NOT let him use you and your body to fulfill his horny needs. Having sex with a guy will NOT make you more popular or help you get a boyfriend. Having sex will make you feel awful inside, not to mention earning you the label of a slut. By that time, he will be dating or flirting with some other naïve girl.

#3 - You have to be FRIENDS FIRST with a guy before you should even consider sleeping with him.

My rule of thumb is to always be FRIENDS FIRST with a guy before considering any type of physical relationship. If you are friends first, then you have a solid foundation on which to build. Stimulate him with your mind and awesome personality, NOT your body. When you start with the physical part first, the relationship NEVER lasts. Your dream guy does not even get a chance to know who you are and all of your wonderful qualities. And if you are too uncomfortable or embarrassed to talk about sex with him, then you should DEFINITELY NOT even consider having it. If you CANNOT talk about what would happen if you got pregnant or if you both have NOT gotten tested for STD's (sexually transmitted diseases), then you are NOT mature enough to have sex. The consequences of having sex are VERY serious. SEX IS A VERY BIG DEAL.

#4 - You ALWAYS have the right to say NO!

There is NEVER a time when you HAVE to do anything that you do NOT want to. If your dream guy gets mad, then he is NOT worth it and does NOT sound so dreamy to me. Date rape, when a guy forces himself physically on you, is a crime. It is a violent act that is usually committed by someone you know or are currently dating. You ALWAYS have the right to change your mind.

In the middle of fooling around, if you change your mind, then he will just have to deal with it. YOU are in control of YOU. Do not ever give your power away to a guy. Use your voice and do NOT be afraid to speak up or fight back. Take a self-defense class to learn how to protect yourself.

NEVER put yourself in a risky situation. Do not EVER let a boy lock the door of the room you are in. Keep the door open, or better yet, stay in a public place and around other people. Try to avoid secluded places, avoid alcohol and drugs, and drive your own car if possible. If you do have a drink wherever you go, make sure that you NEVER leave your drink alone or put it down anywhere. Guys put date rape drugs in girl's drinks to make you feel drunk and lose consciousness. Then they sexually assault you and you may not even remember it. If your date ever gets violent, kick him in the balls, yell, scream, bite, use whatever means you have to in order to get away. Use your cell phone to call 911 for help.

Do NOT get caught up in thinking that if you do not do what he wants, he will not like you or want to go out with you. That is crap! Tell him if he is horny to finish the job himself. Ask him if he has ever met rosy palm?! That is the nice way to tell him that he needs to handle his own horniness. You will be there waiting for him when he is done. Then you can have a great conversation and continue the rest of the night!

#5 - You only have ONE "first time", so make it special.

Almost every girl that I have ever asked about their first time of having sex wishes that she had waited longer. Most people do NOT have good memories about their first sexual experience. That is pretty sad. I have heard too many "wham bam thank you mam" stories, which means that a guy has sex with you and then you never hear from him again. I hope this does not sound familiar to you.

Having sex for the first time should be a wonderful and memorable experience. It should be filled with romance and mature love. It should be with someone who loves you and who is special. It should NOT take place in the back seat of your boyfriend's car or on the front lawn of his house. Do NOT ever let anyone use you for sex. Have self-respect and set your standards high. Make sure your first time is special. Make it a memory that you WANT to remember, not a nightmare that you cannot forget!

#6 - Having sex with a guy who is not your boyfriend will NOT make him want to ask you to be his girlfriend.

I cannot tell you how many times girls have said to me that they had sex with a guy because they thought it would make him like them. UGH! That could not be farther from the truth. Having sex with a guy before becoming his girlfriend, will unfortunately earn you the label of slut. Guys DO NOT want girlfriends who are slutty. Guys want girlfriends who respect themselves and have values. Friends-with-benefits will NOT get you your dream guy. It will, however, get you very depressed. You will end up feeling used and brokenhearted. It will ruin your friendship and make you feel awkward around each other. When you start the relationship with sex, it NEVER goes any farther than that. When you start a relationship with a friendship, it has the chance of becoming something really special.

I have also heard the nasty rumor that having sex will make you more popular and make you fit in. That is crap. Do NOT do something because everyone else does it. Do what you want to do because you love and respect yourself. NEVER let anyone bully or pressure you into something you do NOT want to do. Just because all of your friends have had sex, does NOT mean that you have to. If you have had sex already, it does NOT mean that you have to keep having it.

You can stop today. Do NOT KEEP PUTTING YOURSELF AT RISK. You owe no one else an explanation. You are the one who has to look at yourself in the mirror every single day. Make good choices so you are looking at someone you can be proud of. Life gives us a new chance to start over each and every day. Please take advantage of that opportunity.

#7 - *When you sleep with a guy without using a condom, you are exposing yourself to every disease that he has been exposed to.*

Let's be honest. People lie about how many times they have had sex. They are NOT going to tell you the real number of people they have slept with. Isn't your life and future worth more than some horny lying guy? Is he REALLY worth taking the chance of becoming pregnant or infected with a disease? Most guys do NOT show symptoms of having a sexually transmitted disease. As a result, they NEVER even know that they are infected or that they are infecting someone else. Can you imagine living the rest of your life with herpes or gonorrhea or even worse, dying of AIDS?

The number of teens and adults with sexually transmitted diseases is and has been steadily increasing. Sexually transmitted infections and diseases are illnesses passed from one person to another by vaginal, oral, and anal intercourse, or other foreplay activities. There are more than 30 sexually transmitted diseases. These sexually transmitted diseases can damage your health PERMANENTLY without showing ANY symptoms. Women and girls who are NOT treated and cured might NEVER be able to have children. Certain sexually transmitted diseases can be passed to the fetus during pregnancy and birth and put the baby at risk. Some sexually transmitted diseases can cause a lifetime of health problems or even death. Do NOT become another statistic. Please protect your health and your future. Do NOT ruin your chance for happiness and success for a horny guy.

Now write a letter to yourself about your decisions and goals regarding sex. If you write your values and thoughts down, then you are more likely to follow them. This is just an outline to follow, but please write this letter from your heart and take it seriously. This is YOUR future!

Date:

Dear Me-

I promise that I won't have sex until I _____

_____

When I do have sex, I will _____

_____

When I have sex, I will not _____

_____

I won't ever _____

_____

I promise to _____

_____

Love,

Me

SECRET # 6 –Everyone gets dumped!

You made it all this way only to get dumped. Getting dumped usually happens when you least expect it. If it makes you feel any better, EVERYONE gets dumped at some time in their lives. You can and will survive a breakup. Do not take being dumped personally. Try to look at it as a learning experience. You will not like every guy that likes you and every guy you like will not like you. It was just not meant to be. Sometimes we learn the most valuable lessons as a result of the most painful experiences. This will give you a chance to look back at what happened and figure out what you can do differently next time.

HERE ARE MY SEVEN SIMPLE SOLUTIONS TO GETTING DUMPED:

#1 - There is more than one fish in the sea for everyone.

It may not seem like it when you get dumped, but there is DEFINITELY more than one person for each of us. When your heart is broken, it is hard to imagine that life goes on, but it does. Every day is a new chance to start over. One thing I know for sure is that the sun sets and rises every day. When the sun rises tomorrow it will not seem as bad as it did today. Each day gets easier. In a few weeks or months, you will forget that he even existed. Time heals all wounds.

Soon you will move onto someone better and nicer. If you need some reassurance about this, ask someone you are close to who has had a healthy relationship themselves. I am a firm believer in fate. If it did not work out, then the relationship was not meant to be. You cannot force fate. Who knows? You might get back together someday when the timing is right or you might meet someone who is a better match for you?

Please do NOT be one of those girls who settle for the not-so-Mr. Right because they just want to have a boyfriend. Ugh! You will NEVER meet the guy of your dreams if you are stringing along your not-so-dreamy guy. Have the guts to be alone until you find your dream guy. Good things come to those who wait. Like I always say, "You should be your OWN best company." NEVER depend on anyone else to make YOU happy. You will be glad that you waited when you actually meet your soul mate. He will be your best friend and partner in life. You will share common goals and support each other in following your dreams.

#2 - NEVER let your ex-dream guy know how much he hurt you.

Never give your ex-dream guy the satisfaction of knowing that he hurt you. Move on with your life with your dignity and pride intact. Hold your head high and feel proud of yourself NO MATTER WHAT. Everything happens for a reason- good and bad. The key is to figure out the reason and learn from the experience.

Getting revenge may be an immediate afterthought of being dumped because you want to get back at him for hurting you. However, a public or private display of revenge will just make you look desperate and pitiful. The best revenge you have against being dumped is to move on happily and successfully with your own life. Make him feel like he made the BIGGEST mistake of his life by breaking up with you. Show him what he is missing. Become the best YOU that you can be. Be proud of who you are now and who you will become in the future.

Just remember that your ex-dream guy will NEVER meet anyone like you again. It is truly his loss. You are a uniquely wonderful person and he is the loser, not you. You deserve the BEST life has to offer. Do NOT waste anymore energy living in the past. The sky is the limit and you can accomplish ANYTHING you set your mind to. The recipe for success is to believe in yourself.

#3 – Do NOT wallow in your sorrows.

Breaking up is hard to do, but you WILL get through it. Allow yourself a mourning period of a few weeks at the most. Set aside a "wallowing time" each day for about an hour when you are allowed to wallow. Only during this time are you allowed to cry and be brokenhearted. Then pick a specific date when you will STOP ALL WALLOWING. If you are having trouble not feeling sorry for yourself, volunteer with people who are less fortunate than you. Go to a local hospital and volunteer on the children's floor. Volunteering will quickly make you realize that your life is not so bad after all.

Keep in mind that you will NOT meet anyone else while you are sitting in your room crying your eyes out. Your new dream guy is NOT going to come bang your door down. You have to get off your butt and go find him. Get out there and have some fun. Let your friends and family take you out to distract you from your gloom and doom.

After you are done wallowing, pick a theme song for yourself to listen to every day. Gloria Gaynor's "I will Survive" is always a good choice. Empower yourself and become stronger and wiser. There is NOTHING you cannot conquer. You are a strong, self-confident, smart, and beautiful girl. NEVER let a guy define who you are.

#4 - Pamper yourself ALL day EVERY day.

Just being a girl gives you the right to pamper yourself 24 hours a day 7.days a week. Even if you have not been dumped, you still need to take care of yourself and treat yourself like a princess. If you have recently been dumped, here are some ideas to help you feel brand new again:

- Get a manicure.
- Get a pedicure.
- Get a massage.
- Take a bubble bath and light candles in the bathroom.
- Start a new hobby or sign up for a fun class.
- Rent a funny movie or watch your favorite television show.
- Read a good book.
- Go shopping and buy a new outfit.
- Get a new haircut.
- Join a gym.
- Have a girl's night out with your friends.
- Go for a walk in nature.
- Go to the beach.
- Spend time somewhere beautiful.
- Redecorate your room with positive and inspirational quotes and pictures.
- Write in your journal.
- Express yourself creatively.
- Go to my web site and sign up for a great class or program www.expressyourselftoday.com

Being dumped is a great opportunity to reinvent yourself. Make it a positive experience instead of a negative one. Today is YOUR day, so make the most of it!

#5 - *Act like you have moved on, even if you have not.*

Your ex-dream guy is expecting you to be wallowing at home, crying, depressed and hugging his picture. The WORST thing you could do is to prove him right. Some guys get off on the fact that they are such a powerful force in your life. Right now he is probably thinking that you cannot live without him. Please spare me. Do NOT give away your power so easily. Act like you have moved onto bigger and better things, even if you have not.

NEVER let him see you cry. Keep a stiff upper lip. Cry at home if you have to or in the bathroom. Remember that you are only allowed to cry during your "wallowing time". Do NOT give him the satisfaction of thinking about him for one more minute of your life. He is CLEARLY not worth it. Get out there and meet other dream guys. Go out with guys who are just friends. Make sure your ex sees you out on the town. Even if your heart is broken into a million tiny pieces, get up and go out. Put one foot in front of the other and each day will get easier. Trust me. I have been through it more times than I want to remember. Tell all of your friends that you are over him and have moved on.

Make a list below of ALL of the things you did NOT like about your ex-not-so-dreamy guy:

1-

2-

3-

4-

5-

Take this list out any time you start getting weepy about your ex. Keep reminding yourself that he is totally NOT worth it. After all, do you think he is sitting at home crying about you? Yeah right!

#6 - Analyze what went wrong.

Once you are over the initial shock and sadness of breaking up, take some time and really analyze what went wrong. Do NOT rush right into dating someone else immediately after getting dumped. You need time to talk and think about what happened. You are on the rebound and do not have a clear head yet. Do NOT try to fill your sadness and loneliness with someone else. True happiness comes from within yourself.

Spend some time alone and do some serious soul searching. Then answer the following questions:

- Do you love yourself?

- Were you friends first before becoming girlfriend and boyfriend?

- Why did you and he break up?

- How long did you go out with each other?

- What did you fight over?

- Did you get along with each other's friends?

- Did you get along with each other's family?

- Did you change at all during the relationship?

- Was your relationship like your parents' relationship? Often times we mirror our parents' relationship, which can be good or bad. Something to think about.

- What was your part in the break-up?

- What types of things did you do together?

- Did he fit your profile of your dream guy? Why or why not? Be specific.

- What will you do differently in your next relationship?

- What did you learn from this relationship?

Sometimes the most painful experiences are the ones we learn the most from. If you jump from relationship to relationship, then you will never have the opportunity to figure out what happened. In some cases, you may have done nothing wrong. At least take some time to ponder over the whole experience. We create patterns of behavior in our lives that keep repeating themselves until we realize they exist. The first step to positive change is awareness that you have a problem. Do you always date the same type of guy? Does he treat you nice? Does he come from a healthy family? There are many factors to consider in a dream guy, other than the fact that he is cute!

#7 – *Put the past behind you and plan for a better and brighter future!*

Every relationship needs closure. Go find a big cardboard box. Now collect everything he ever gave you and dump it all in the box. And I mean EVERYTHING-pictures, clothes, jewelry, notes, etc. Go get some masking tape and write his name on it. Now tape up the box and put it in the attic. Some day you might want to go through it for old time's sake. You cannot move forward when you are still living in the past. Let go and move on. If it makes you feel any better, save one picture to put up on your dartboard and get some anger out. Bombs away! This is a very therapeutic activity☺. You need to get all of those negative feelings out of your system in a healthy way.

Sometimes during a breakup you might not get all of your questions answered and you might never have a chance to say everything that you needed to say. Take out a piece of paper and write him a letter. Do NOT hold back and really write how you feel. Let it rip! You can mail it if you choose to or you can just shred it afterwards. Just the act of writing the letter brings closure, even if he never reads it. If you decide to mail it, who knows, you might get the closure you need directly from him or maybe not. At least you are getting all of your feelings off your chest in a positive way.

Now you are ready to leave the past and your ex-dream guy behind. It is time to focus on what is REALLY important in life and that is YOU, YOUR dreams, YOUR goals, and YOUR bright future ahead, with or without a guy. Life is a gift and the opportunities are endless. Get up and go for it!

SECRET # 7 – Be happy alone!

My motto has ALWAYS been and will continue to be that it is better to be happy and alone than with someone and miserable. Do NOT have a boyfriend just for the sake of having a boyfriend. As I said in the beginning of the book, you MUST learn how to love yourself and be happy with yourself FIRST before you can EVER be happy with anyone else. That is why so many relationships fail and the divorce rate is over 50%. People are trying to fill the emptiness and unhappiness within themselves through having a relationship with someone else. That NEVER EVER works.

Your happiness needs to come from within YOU. Nobody else can make YOU happy. Your goal should be to fully develop yourself and become independent before joining your life with someone else. When you are old enough, it is a great experience to live alone before getting married. Get to know who you are and learn how to be happy alone. After high school, you should be focusing on getting the education you need to get your DREAM JOB. This is YOUR time to travel anywhere your heart desires and take some DREAM VACATIONS. The world is an oyster just waiting to be discovered. This is YOUR time to discover all of YOUR hidden talents and passions. You have the REST of your life to get married and have a family. Talk to anyone who is married and they will tell you the exact same thing. Once you have your own family, then most of your time and money goes to them, not you. Now is YOUR time. Take advantage of this wonderful opportunity for self-discovery. Learn to live your life for YOU, not for a dream guy, your family or your friends.

HERE ARE MY SEVEN SIMPLE SOLUTIONS TO BEING HAPPY & ALONE:

#1 - Live YOUR life to the fullest!

Live every day as if it was your last. Carpe diem~ seize the day. Be productive. Stop and smell the roses. Make the world a better place. Give back to society. Set goals for your life. You NEVER want to look back on your life and have regrets. You do NOT want to be one of those people that go through life saying "I could have, should have, would have, but DID NOT". Always appreciate life and be grateful for what YOU have.

Make a list of things you would like to accomplish at each age of your life:

5 or more things I want to do before I am 20 years old:

1-

2-

3-

4-

5-

5 or more things I want to do before I am 30 years old:

1-

2-

3-

4-

5-

Eventually write a list in your journal for age 40, 50, and so on. It is really fun to look back on the goals you set for yourself as you get older. Successful, happy and high-achieving people are goal-setters.

#2 - Reach for the stars!

Anything is possible. NEVER limit yourself. The only real limitations are the ones you create for yourself. Your power is unlimited. If YOU believe YOU can do it, YOU will. The higher you set your goals, the more you will achieve. The more you expect, the more you will get. Do not let ANYONE stand in your way, no matter who they are. I once had a professor in graduate school tell me that I was too goal-oriented and peppy. I have since nicknamed myself the "Peppy Professor"☺. This clearly was HER issue, not mine. Good thing that I was smart enough to realize that SHE was the one with the problem or I might have taken her criticism seriously. Ladies, let me tell you that there is NO such thing as being too goal-oriented and peppy! I hope she buys this book and eats her words.

This is a great example of the fact that MOST people will NOT be supportive of your goals and dreams, including your friends and family. MOST people are too unhappy with their own lives to be happy for someone else. They want to drag you down with them. You have to listen to YOUR own inner voice and be YOUR own cheerleader. As long as you believe in YOURSELF, nothing else matters. All you need is you. NEVER give up and ALWAYS reach for the stars.

#3 – *Constantly set goals.*

The process of goal-setting helps you choose what you want to achieve in life. Setting life goals increases your motivation and builds your self-esteem and self-confidence. You will not achieve anything if you do not set goals for yourself. How can you do something if you do not know what it is you want to do? You will just drift through life and let life happen to you. Instead, you need to let YOU happen to life.

Setting goals helps you make the most of your life. High-achievers in all fields of life know how to set goals. They know what they want and they know how to get there. They let NOTHING stand in their way. YOU can do the same thing.

Below write out 3 goals that you want to achieve in the next 3 months, 6 months and 1 year:

Goals to achieve in 3 months:

1-

2-

3-

Goals to achieve in 6 months:

1-

2-

3-

Goals to achieve in 1 year:

1-

2-

3-

Go back to your goal list and write down next to each goal HOW you are going to achieve it. Every goal needs a plan of action to go with it. Make your goals achievable by making them realistic. Setting short-term and long-term goals is an effective way to measure your progress and success. Keep checking on your progress and revise your action plan as needed.

#4 – Be selfishly smart.

Always put yourself FIRST. As a girl, sometimes that is not an easy thing to do. You are taught at an early age that women are caregivers and nurturers to everyone else. You might see the women around you not taking good care of themselves. Please do NOT make this mistake. Do not become a martyr, which means that you take care of everyone BUT yourself. YOUR first responsibility as a girl is to be selfishly smart by taking care of you FIRST. Then you can help the other people in your life. You must learn how to nurture your OWN body, mind and spirit first. You will be NO good to anyone else if you are NOT nurturing yourself. This is a VERY important life lesson to learn, the sooner the better for you.

One day you might get married and have children. When you have a list of responsibilities a mile long, it is hard to focus on yourself. You need to fill yourself up FIRST before you can give to others. If you do not, then you will have nothing left to give. It is like filling up the gas tank of a car. If you do not fill up the tank, then it cannot run. There is nothing MORE important than YOU. NEVER put anyone else before you, especially a guy. You need to be #1- ALL day EVERY day.

#5 - NEVER settle for anything LESS than the BEST!

You deserve the BEST life has to offer. You are AWESOME! When you have great expectations, they will lead to great results. Set the bar high. Once you truly love yourself, you will NOT expect anything LESS from anyone else, especially a guy. The more you develop yourself the happier and healthier you will be. Then you will attract other happy and healthy people. ANYONE that wants to be part of your life will have to honor your requests. You deserve to be treated like precious gold by your dream guy or anyone else in your life.

If life gives you lemons, then start making lemonade. You only have ONE life to live. YOU have to be in control. NEVER give away your control to someone else. This is YOUR life, NOT theirs. Let them live their own life. Life is not always easy, but YOU are in charge of what happens. If there is a problem, then YOU have to be the one to fix it. Be optimistic and positive. If your family and friends do NOT support you and are NOT positive, then find some new people that are positive and supportive. Life is too short to let other people bring you down. ALWAYS keep in mind that the most important supporter and cheerleader in your life is YOU. You go girl!

#6 –Become your ultimate self!

Whatever it is that you fear the most is what you need to put FIRST on your to-do list. Your fears are great indicators of the hurdles you need to conquer in order to become your ultimate self. You are on your own special journey through life. Once you face your fears head-on, you are UNSTOPPABLE and your self-esteem will grow by leaps and bounds. There is NOTHING you cannot learn or do. Just believe in yourself. Once you overcome your fears, the sky is the limit.

I am not very fond of heights, so I decided to face my fear by going skydiving. This was truly one of the BEST experiences of my life. I am SO glad that I did it. It taught me that I can do whatever I set my mind to and that I can work through my fears. Skydiving made me a better and stronger person. Skydiving also increased my self-esteem and motivated me to set my goals even higher. I would never go skydiving again because I did it once. I can now say that I did it and have the video to prove it, and so can you!

#7 - ALWAYS LOVE YOURSELF NO MATTER WHAT!

No matter what happens in your life, the BEST gift you can give to yourself is self-love. All you need is YOU. Respect yourself and others will respect you. NEVER listen to negative or critical people. Surround yourself with people who will cheer you on and lift up your spirits. Most people do NOT have vision and dreams. Many people let fear stand in their way. Do not become one of those people. Life is WAY too short to live it for someone else.

If you want to become a doctor and you have good grades and the skills necessary to become one, then do NOT let anyone discourage you. If you want to become an actress and you have the talent to do so, NEVER let anyone talk you out of your dreams because they do NOT think that it is practical. If your dad is a lawyer and wants you to become a lawyer, you do NOT have to, if that is not what YOU want. Follow your dreams, not someone else's. I have always said that if there is a WILL, there is a WAY to achieve it. If you want something bad enough, you will find a way to accomplish it. Follow your inner voice and honor what it tells you to do. Be proud of who you are today and who you will become in the future!

You are the one who looks yourself in the mirror every day. Live your life so you are PROUD of who is staring back at you.

Develop your own personal mission statement by answering the following questions:

Who is the REAL you?

What is your TRUE purpose in life?

What is your inner voice telling YOU to do?

What is YOUR passion?

How will YOU achieve your purpose and passion?

Why were YOU put on this earth?

Now flip back to the beginning of this book and read it all over again. Keep reading it until you have the entire book memorized. Learn it, live it, and breathe it. Tell EVERY girl you know to go to her computer right now and buy this book at www.buybooksontheweb.com.

TOGETHER we can educate, motivate and empower a whole new generation of self-confident girls. YOU are the bright future of our world. Every time YOU respect and honor yourself, you are respecting and honoring EVERY woman of the world. Keep the momentum going. Carpe diem~ Seize the day!

"Unwritten"

I am unwritten
Can't read my mind
I'm undefined
I'm just beginning
The pen's in my hand
Ending unplanned
Staring at the blank page before you
Open up the dirty window
Let the sun illuminate the words you cannot find
Reaching for something in the distance
So close you can almost taste it
Release your inhibitions
Feel the rain on your skin
No one else can feel it for you
Only YOU can let it in
No one else, no one else can
speak the words on your lips
Drench yourself in words unspoken
Live your life with arms wide open
Today is where your book begins
The rest is still unwritten
I break tradition
Sometimes my tries
Are outside the lines
We've been conditioned
To not make mistakes
But I can't live that way
Staring at the blank page before you
Open up the dirty window
Let the sun illuminate the words that you cannot find
Reaching for something in the distance
So close you can almost taste it
Release your inhibitions!

~Song Lyrics written by Natasha Bedingfield, Danielle Brisebois,
Wayne Rodrigues. From the CD "Unwritten".

79